Jo Eades performs regularly on the Bristol spoken word scene. In 2023, she performed on the Milk Poetry stage at Valleyfest and was selected as one of eight emerging poets from the South West to be part of Apple and Snakes' Future Voices project. In 2024 she was the Lyra Bristol Poetry Slam Champion and won the Hip Yak Poetry Shack Slam at WOMAD Festival. In 2025 she featured at Keynsham Music Festival, won the Ledbury Poetry Festival Slam and came fourth in the England SLAM! Championships.

She has been featured four times on BBC Radio Bristol's Upload, being one of their 'best of' poets for 2024.

Jo Eades

Flanked

Burning Eye

Contents

Last Times

No one warns you
one day she'll prefer
a bottle to your breast, rather
go on holiday with friends, want
cash for Christmas, not a stocking.

Nobody whispered in my ear
there'd be a last time I'd
lick chocolate icing off the wooden spoon,
have homemade jam in my pantry,
hold my mother's hand.

Newborn

You're

A sponge
washed over by waves
of motion, absorbing
an ocean of stimuli.

A coral
of such intense colour,
seemingly robust but
vulnerable to the slightest touch.

I'm

A swimmer
caught in a riptide,
being dragged out to sea,
adrift offshore.

A diver
out of my depth,
frantically treading water
for fear I hurt what is most precious.

Achievement

The truth is, I'd always disappointed her.
But that pram said it all. A relic
that stood in the cupboard under the stairs:
testament to the ultimate, unforgivable failing.
Might as well get rid of this,
won't be needed again in this family.
I looked away,
didn't reply.

Now here you are,
tangible human form in my arms,
who did nothing
but feed off my body, survive and grow,
yet outshine anything I've ever done
or likely ever will.

If I Believed in God, I'd Pray

For the Lord to teach me not to:

Expect her to fulfil my unaccomplished dreams; they are my failings.
Judge her by the standards of my day, for they belong in the past.
Use that phrase *do as I say*, but guide with wisdom.
Burden her with pressure, but enable her to grow.
Start sounding like my mother; it isn't my destiny.
Ignore my mother; she isn't always wrong.

For the Lord to teach me to:

Listen to the words behind *I'm fine*; they are just waiting for the right question.
Tune in to her frequency, when every radio is blaring Radio 4.
Notice the little things that don't make sense; they add up.
Trust my maternal intuition; it's what it's there for.
Embrace her flaws; they'll balance her brilliance.
Forgive her trespasses; it's payback time.

My New Working Week

Monday / today I take my child to baby group at the community centre / attempt to converse with women / young enough to be my children / who appear to have given birth to their brains along with their placentas / Last week a boy literally sat on my baby / this week I might sit on him

Tuesday / I spend the morning at Waterbabies / in a pool designed for geriatrics / submerging my baby / not long out of a lifetime in water / to teach her a lesson in not drowning / She will thank me for this in later years

Wednesday / we go to soft play / where I watch her frolic in a pit of plastic balls coated in streptococcus / emerge smelling like a urinal / When we get home / I boil wash her clothes / resist the urge to scrub her raw with bleach

Thursday / we attend Sing and Sign / where I mime ridiculous gestures / to rhymes that will plague my head all week / and wonder if the joy of seeing my child tell me / without words / that she wants yet another biscuit / is worth this public humiliation / She will give me that look / which I will see more of in her teens / which says / without words / *Mum, you're an embarrassment*

Friday / I will not leave the house / make myself a Yorkshire brew / turn on *Women's Hour* / watch as my child sleeps / basking in adoration / breathe

Ontogeny (Initiation)

I was probably in denial.
Clueless and unprepared.
Hadn't read the next chapter.
But you came anyway
and, like a rabbit in headlights,
those piercing eyes gave me a look
as if to say
Take care of me.

So I wiped your eyes
and I wiped your hands
and I wiped your bottom
and I wiped your projectile vomit off the walls.

And you just did all that stuff
you're hardwired to do;
you crawled and you bawled
you walked and you talked.
I tell you –
it was amazing.

And I picked you up when you fell
and hurt your knee;
I told you it would be okay.
And it was.

My Daughter Said

after John Hegley

Mum, you are old,
but friends at school
think you're cool
and they'd pay
to dye their hair
your countless shades of grey.

And though you don't know
what I mean
by a meme
you've been
round the block
and seen
things that would shock
those naïve mums.

They may be young and in their prime,
but where are the lines
of life and laughter
round their eyes?

They may be young and in their prime,
but you shine
and you're mine.
I am proud
and I own you.

And I said,
What do you mean, old?

Elegy for the Puppies

A poster in the school corridor reads,
Every time an apostrophe is misused, a puppy dies.

Puppies, dead puppies,
strewn across College Green,
splattered over Park Street,
floating lifeless in the docks.
You careless, murderous children.

Despicable Me

I used to feel I spent half my life in the kitchen.
Chopping, cooking, clearing up;
wanted to feed you well, nourish you.

I wish I'd just fed you beans on toast now and then.
Spoiled us both with a TV dinner.
Sacrificed a good meal for quality time.

I might have noticed cracks, heard silent cries,
well hidden behind long sleeves
and sweatshirts in summer.

Wish I'd spent more time snuggled on the sofa,
feasting in front of the telly.
Watched the whole of *Despicable Me*.

Ontogeny (Maturation)

And when we were in that caravan
that day it just rained and rained
we never got out of our pyjamas
and we danced to Lily Allen for five hours
because it was the only tape there was.

And sometimes you'd leave for school
in yellow dinosaur earrings
and football shorts
and I'd want to shout down the street,
Oi, you forgot to get dressed!

And when you did that thing
I tried not to judge
or blame.
I did what I could
to understand.

Ruth

I watched you, as a toddler,
playing with your toy tea set,
offering my mum a plate of assembled delights.
Lovely, thank you! Shall I eat this now?
Your concerned response,
No, Granny, they're plastic!

How early in life we learn to swap roles,
start caring for the carers.

When exactly did the tide turn?
When I first made her dinner,
offered to drive,
took her arm to cross the road?
As I turned her over
to wash her nether regions,
bed-stricken, she quipped,
I bet you never thought you'd be doing this!

A teenager now, you make a real pot of tea –
ever thoughtful –
but I flinch
as you go to pour and say,
I'll be Mum.

You'll Miss Me

When did I start sounding like my mother?
When I suggested you wore a coat to go outside,
even though I'd spent winters at school
in short-sleeved shirts
never feeling the cold?

Or when I asked if you wanted to come out for a walk
(spend some time together, talk),
you echoing the replies I used to give:
No, thanks, Mum, I'm fine.

You see, I wish I'd said yes sometimes now,
feigned interest in cousins I could barely remember.

I would trade all those wasted hours
sat in my room,
the wanderings from fridge to pantry –
I'd walk the lanes, subjected
to her tales of jam and Jerusalem,
just to hear her voice.

Ontogeny (Fruition)

And it's like one day
I just woke up
and the child was gone.
There you were
with breasts and bleeds
and your own ideas
and, exciting as it was,
I felt bereft.

And they say the years race by
and you won't know
where the time's gone
and they're not wrong.
Blink and you miss it.
You grew up, I grew old;
you grew into my clothes,
I shrank into yours.

Now you're making plans,
and you want to go far –
you have all that life ahead of you,
laughs and loves and trials and pain.
If truth be told
I am a bit envious.

But I would have failed
if you didn't want to go.

And you will go far,
you will fly   you will soar.
I will watch, wave –
and I will miss you.

Reconciliation

I bought my mother a card
of two people hugging,
and in it I wrote
in my neatest handwriting
all those things I hadn't said;
not just the easy ones,
the feel-good ones,
the love-you ones
but the hard ones,
the honest ones,
the we-don't-have-to-forgive ones.
I posted it first-class.

And when I saw her next,
lying in that bed,
I held her hand.
We didn't need to speak of it.

Some weeks after she'd gone,
Dad handed me back the card:
opened and resealed, pristine.
I didn't want to upset her, he said.

Grief

At a theatre, you choose your seat.
Avoid the front row. Too close.
Raised stage, crooked neck.

At a funeral, there's a pecking order;
have to earn your place.
The best are those of close family members.

Guaranteed front row.
Close enough to smell the flowers.
Where the action is.

Skipping

She left me all her jewellery.
Engagement ring, eternity ring,
rings for all occasions;
rings making proclamations
of love, commitment, longevity –
testament to years of duty,
perseverance, loyalty.

I don't suppose you'll want them, she said,
and we both knew she was right –
that she'd actually meant *need*.

Tucked away among winter knits,
encased in bubble wrap
and disappointment,
they sit, patiently waiting
to be passed down the line.

Healing

There is a kind of memory that feels like an incision.

So clean and pure and incisive that,
for a second,
it doesn't even hurt.

Then the pain of recollection rushes in;
blood drains, faintness overwhelms.

Time heals, like broken skin,
but months later, reminders

– like nerves still trapped in scar tissue –

will twinge.

Demanding to be scratched.

Reunion

The Cornish coastline,
designated Area of Outstanding Natural Beauty.
Sections so peppered with benches
bearing inscriptions of loved ones departed
they resemble a graveyard.
One is rusting wrought iron; another is rotting wood.
Memories of their namesakes eroding
with the passage of time.

You don't have a bench
(although you are equally deserving of a place).
Yet it's here,

not in the cold ground of some far-off county
but here, that I see you
standing ankle-deep at the water's edge.
Picture that tartan Thermos flask.
Taste the jam sandwiches laced with grains of sand.
Hear you in the muffled shrieks of distant children,
smell you on the warm southerly breeze,
feel you in the sea spray as it hits my face.

I can almost hear your voice.

Yes, you can find me here;
it was my second home.
A million miles from the flatlands of Norfolk
yet visited annually like a pilgrimage.

And I see the waves lapping your ankles now,
hear you echo the words I uttered then:
don't go out too deep!
My, how she's grown.

History repeats like the sea flanks the shore.
Maybe all girls become their mothers,
though I know you'd hate me for saying so.

Don't be sad.
I'm still watching out for you.
It's what we do.

Spare Place

My mother, I answer, as you help me
lay the handed-down kitchen table
bought for half a crown in the fifties

that she would spend hours
scrubbing with a hard-bristled brush,
bucket of soapy water to hand,

drawers my brothers would push
with their knees from the opposite side
to catch me in the stomach,

with that small gouged-out hole
that appeared from nowhere
that none of us owned up to.

*If you could have anyone
join us for dinner,
who would it be?* you ask.

Dancing in the Coruscations

Ash is the residue left after burning:
inorganic, dry, grey byproduct.
So dull, lifeless.
I hope that cardboard scatter tube,
so absurdly buried, has rotted
and let her make her way.

Some say the essence of loved ones lingers.
Dust is fine, solid specks – light and floaty.
In households, primarily dead skin cells.
When you – my girl – leave, back up north again,
I like to think you're still at home.
I waft an occasional feather duster
and, as sun pours in through the windows,
I see you dancing in the coruscations.

The Quies

I am again drawn back to this place:
sit on this monument
of Cornish slate and cement
In memory of Nick
where years ago, I once sat
to breastfeed my baby.

Staring across the sea to the Quies,
absence is an ache
like the one in my hips
that worsens with each coastal walk.

I wonder if I return
to remind myself of loss,
like stabbing my leg
with a compass at school
to stop from falling asleep.

This expanse before me
shimmering in the sunlight
is like the void
I can embrace.
Or drown in.

Time for me to leave,
move on,
just as they both have now.
I knew they would.

Ebb and Flow

And there will be days when
you still need me
and days when
I will not cross your mind.

Though sand will shift beneath our feet,
each tide forging new landscapes,
I'll always be there   watching out
somewhere in the dunes.

Left

When you go back to uni, you leave a mess.
Oil-clagged paintbrushes stand pointlessly
in a glass of water on the table.
An almost empty packet of pizza-flavoured crisps
waits abandoned on your bed.
Socks, cast off, everywhere, desperately
search for their significant other.

A team of coffee mugs have congregated
around your essays, forming a think tank.
The house is a war zone of discarded earrings,
hiding in carpets, poised to impale.
Yesterday's pants fester on your bedroom floor.
Did your mother teach you nothing?

When you've gone a calm seeps in,
under the door, through the ill-fitting window frames.
Women's Hour discusses loneliness and loss.
6 Music plays 'Hit the Road Jack'.
The fridge exclaims,
We're no longer out of milk!
The pantry looks accusingly;
Who's going to eat this tricolore pasta now?
The raptor, who used to hide round the corner
waiting to pounce, has gone into hibernation
in the cupboard under the stairs.

The landing light turns itself off at night.
The front door locks itself.
The rooms grow a little,
the clock ticks slower, louder.
The aroma of youth has departed
for the station, to dance again – up north.

Now plastic-handled cutlery designed for small hands
remains, but has no place.
Primary school artwork that adorns the toilet wall
has faded and frayed.
There are no crayons under the sofa.
The Nutella jar is full.
The house whimpers softly, creaks in its spaces.

In another city, up the M5, a bedroom floor
can barely be seen for charity shop apparel.
A desk supports university library books,
blocks in a never-ending game of Jenga.
A kitchen hosts a huddle of saucepans,
forever in a state of soak.
Another can of Guinness is opened.

Forest Bathing in Herefordshire

The Tripadvisor review claimed it'd be a mindful experience
and curiosity sent us on the short walk to the woods
through the cows in the field, it had forgotten to mention.

A colourful canvas announced itself, strung between trees:
a tent in a former life, perhaps, though sheltering under it now
would obscure the leaves, missing the point.

Instead, we rolled ourselves onto the makeshift platform,
meeting in the middle like a clam closing,
our size eight boots knocking together.

Attempted to be appreciative of nature –
contemplative, grown-up,
but when the strings snapped and we plummeted

the few feet to the ground, I was mindful only
of our tears, gushing like geysers.
How I love your laugh!

Acknowledgements

My heartfelt thanks to:

Stefan Mohamed for his Find Your Poetic Voice courses during lockdown, which kickstarted this journey, and Tim Liardet, my tutor on the creative writing MA at Bath Spa University, for encouraging me to stick with it.

The lovely people of the Bristol spoken word scene for your welcome and support, and Raise the Bar, Milk Poetry, Satellite of Love and Tonic for providing a platform on which to share my work.

Tom Sastry, Tom Denbigh and Malaika Kegode, who read *Flanked* with a poetic eye. Thank you for your generosity of time, talent and spirit.

Frankie Coltman, Alice Washbourne and Helen Timbrell, who read it as browsers in a second-hand bookshop. Your comments were invaluable.

Stefan Mohamed, Malaika Kegode, Jon Seagrave, Tom Denbigh and Adam Crowther for your kind words for the back cover.

And lastly, Clive Birnie at Burning Eye Books for having the faith to put my spoken words into print, and everyone who gives up their time to read them.

I am truly grateful to you all.

www.ingramcontent.com/pod-product-compliance
Lightning Source LLC
Chambersburg PA
CBHW021946040426
42448CB00008B/1268